DOCUMENT ANALYSIS

SOLVING CRIMES WITH SCIENCE:
Forensics

DOCUMENT ANALYSIS

Elizabeth Bauchner

Mason Crest

Mason Crest
450 Parkway Drive, Suite D
Broomall, PA 19008
www.masoncrest.com

Printed and bound in the United States of America.

First printing
9 8 7 6 5 4 3 2 1

Series ISBN: 978-1-4222-2861-6
ISBN: 978-1-4222-2865-4
ebook ISBN: 978-1-4222-8951-8

The Library of Congress has cataloged the
hardcopy format(s) as follows:

Library of Congress Cataloging-in-Publication Data

Bauchner, Elizabeth.
  Document analysis / Elizabeth Bauchner.
     p. cm. — (Solving crimes with science, forensics)
  Audience: 012.
  Audience: Grades 7 to 8.
  Includes bibliographical references and index.
  ISBN 978-1-4222-2865-4 (hardcover) — ISBN 978-1-4222-2861-6 (series) — ISBN 978-1-4222-8951-8
(ebook)
  1. Forgery—Juvenile literature. 2. Graphology—Juvenile literature. 3. Forensic sciences—Juvenile
literature. I. Title.
  HV6675.B382 2014
  363.25'65—dc23
                                        2013006936

Produced by Vestal Creative Services.
www.vestalcreative.com

Contents

Introduction

By Jay A. Siegel, Ph.D.
Director, Forensic and Investigative Sciences Program
Indiana University, Purdue University, Indianapolis

It seems like every day the news brings forth another story about crime in the United States. Although the crime rate has been slowly decreasing over the past few years (due perhaps in part to the aging of the population), crime continues to be a very serious problem. Increasingly, the stories we read that involve crimes also mention the role that forensic science plays in solving serious crimes. Sensational crimes provide real examples of the power of forensic science. In recent years there has been an explosion of books, movies, and TV shows devoted to forensic science and crime investigation. The wondrously successful *CSI* TV shows have spawned a major increase in awareness of and interest in forensic science as a tool for solving crimes. *CSI* even has its own syndrome: the "*CSI* Effect," wherein jurors in real cases expect to hear testimony about science such as fingerprints, DNA, and blood spatter because they saw it on TV.

The unprecedented rise in the public's interest in forensic science has fueled demands by students and parents for more educational programs that teach the applications of science to crime. This started in colleges and universities but has filtered down to high schools and middle schools. Even elementary school students now learn how science is used in the criminal justice system. Most educators agree that this developing interest in forensic science is a good thing. It has provided an excellent opportunity to teach students science—and they have fun learning it! Forensic science is an ideal vehicle for teaching science for several reasons. It is truly multidisciplinary; practically every field of science has forensic applications. Successful forensic scientists must be good problem solvers and critical thinkers. These are critical skills that all students need to develop.

In all of this rush to implement forensic science courses in secondary schools throughout North America, the development of grade-appropriate resources that help guide students and teachers is seriously lacking. This new series: *Solving Crimes With Science: Forensics* is important and timely. Each book in the series contains a concise, age-appropriate discussion of one or more areas of forensic science.

Students are never too young to begin to learn the principles and applications of science. Forensic science provides an interesting and informative way to introduce scientific concepts in a way that grabs and holds the students' attention. *Solving Crimes With Science: Forensics* promises to be an important resource in teaching forensic science to students twelve to eighteen years old.

back alive
$2000
tomorrow
at 10:00 a.m.
the park
$8.20
$4.20
$5.20
$7.00
$4.05
$29 1/2
$4.40
$0.60

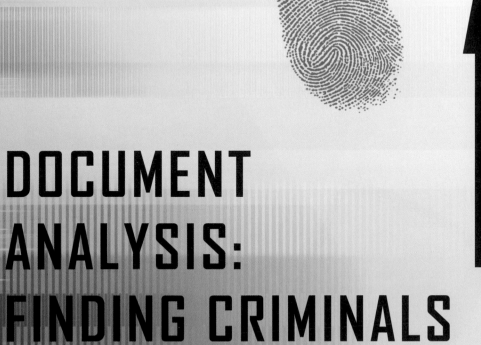

DOCUMENT ANALYSIS: FINDING CRIMINALS

On July 4, 1956, Betty Weinberger placed her one-month-old son Peter in his baby carriage on the patio of her Westbury, New York, home. She then stepped inside for a few minutes while he slept. When she returned to check on her son, all she found was an empty baby carriage and a ransom note asking for $2,000.

The kidnapper, later identified through his handwriting on the ransom note as Angelo LaMarca, apologized for his actions but said he needed the money. LaMarca promised the baby would be brought back "safe and happy" the following day if his demand was met, but he threatened to kill the baby at the "first wrong move."

Despite the kidnapper's threats, Betty Weinberger immediately called the Nassau County Police Department. Peter's father, Morris Weinberger, requested that newspapers hold off on the story, and all but one newspaper granted his request; the following day the *New York Daily News* ran a front-page story.

That same day, news reporters swarmed the area where the kidnapper was supposed to bring the baby and pick up the ransom money. Police left a phony ransom package, but LaMarca never appeared. Six days after the kidnapping, on July 10, the kidnapper called the Weinberger home two

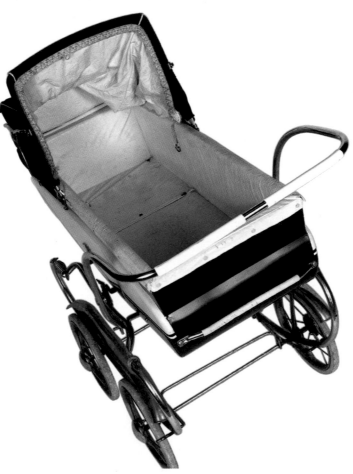

Investigators were led to the kidnapper of one-month-old Peter Weinberger by the ransom note left in the baby carriage.

separate times with instructions on where to leave the money, but he didn't show up at either location. Police found another handwritten note at the second drop-off location telling the parents where to find Peter if "everything goes smooth."

On July 11, seven days after the kidnapping, the **Federal Bureau of Investigation (FBI)** got involved in the case and immediately set to work comparing the handwriting in the ransom note to the handwriting in the second note found at the drop-off location. These two notes were the only sources of evidence they had. They enlisted the help of handwriting experts from the FBI Crime Laboratory in Washington, D.C., and these experts quickly trained the FBI special agents on the case in handwriting analysis. The team then set to work.

First, the special agents determined that the handwriting was the same in the two notes. Then they set to work comparing the handwriting in the notes to handwriting samples maintained by the New York State Motor Vehicle Bureau, federal and state **probation** offices, schools, aircraft plants, and various municipalities. On August 22, 1956, after examining and eliminating almost two million handwriting samples, an agent found a similarity between the handwriting on the ransom notes and handwriting in the probation file of Angelo LaMarca.

Investigators quickly discovered that LaMarca was a taxi dispatcher and truck driver who lived in Brooklyn with his wife and two children. He lived in a house he couldn't afford, he had many unpaid bills, and he was being threatened by a loan shark. On August 23, 1956, FBI agents and Nassau County Police arrested LaMarca at his home. At first he denied the kidnapping, but later confessed when presented with the handwriting samples.

He told investigators that on July 4 he had found himself driving around Westbury trying to figure out how he was going to get the money he needed, when he happened upon the Weinberger home and saw Betty Weinberger leaving her baby on the patio. He quickly scribbled a ransom note, snatched Peter, and drove off. The next day, he went to the drop-off site with Peter in the car, but he was scared off by all the press and police. On the way home, he abandoned the baby alive in some bushes off a highway exit.

When FBI Investigators searched the area where LaMarca claimed to have left the baby, they first found a diaper pin—and then the decomposed remains of Peter Weinberger. The grueling search was over.

Forensic What?

According to the American Academy of Forensic Sciences, forensic science, or criminalistics, is "the study and practice of the application of science to the purposes of the law." Forensic literally means characteristic of or suitable for a court of law, while science is the acquisition of knowledge gleaned from direct observation. Skilled forensic document examiners study evidence through what is known as the "scientific method."

So what is the scientific method? According to authors Joe Nickell and John F. Fischer in Crime Science: Methods of Forensic Detection, the scientific method involves analysis (studying the unknown item to determine its essential characteristics), comparison (examining how the characteristics compare with the established properties of known items), and evaluation (assessing the similarities and dissimilarities for identification purposes). It is open-ended, meaning it is open to having its errors corrected in the light of new evidence.

Forensic scientists can expose forgery through intricate analysis of a document.

Peter Weinberger's kidnapping case is just one of dozens of kinds of crimes in which the handwriting of the criminal comes into play. The ransom notes in Peter's case, like all documents used in a crime, are part of a branch of forensic science known *as document analysis or the examination of questioned documents.*

Document examiners are forensic scientists who are called in to assist detectives with criminal investigations that involve documents of all kinds. Their primary work involves any of the following:

- establishing that a document is genuine
- exposing *forgery* in the forms of alterations, additions, or deletions
- identifying individuals through handwriting samples (called standards)
- providing testimony in court when required

Ransom notes are relatively rare documents in the world of crime; the majority of crimes involving questioned documents are not nearly as gripping as kidnappings. Common crimes involving documents include forged checks and counterfeit currency, phony identification papers or concert tickets, altered ledgers, and disputed legal documents such as wills. In some cases, people have created fake manuscripts or diaries of famous people to sell for a lot of money. Even the personal diaries or journals of suspected criminals can be held as evidence during a criminal investigation.

Handwriting analysis, as in the Weinberger case, is only one aspect of document analysis, though it is the most common (along with forgery detection). However, not all questioned documents in a criminal investigation are handwritten. Examination of documents in order to detect forgeries also includes analysis of hand printing, typewriting, commercial printing, and photocopies. Even the documents from typewriters and photocopy machines can be traced back to a particular machine, because over time, these machines devclop their own unique characteristics.

Finally, document analysis also includes examination of the actual papers and inks to establish authenticity of a document in question and to detect alterations or obliterations. For example, document examiners can use special equipment such as ultraviolet light (to be discussed more in chapters 4 and 5) to check watermarks and to see if eraser marks, correction fluid, mismatched inks, or other suspicious alterations have been made to the document.

Catch Me If You Can

In 2002, director Steven Spielberg released the film *Catch Me If You Can*, based on the true story of a young con-man named Frank Abagnale Jr. Abagnale managed to evade the FBI for years while cashing more than $2.5 million in phony checks and masquerading as a pilot, a doctor, and a lawyer. The movie shows just how Abagnale (played by Leonardo DiCaprio) created the fake checks and how the FBI finally caught him.

Handwriting Analysis

Handwriting, like a fingerprint, is unique. Nevertheless, it is far more difficult to identify a person through his handwriting than through his fingerprints. For one thing, fingerprints don't change over time, while handwriting does. Also, criminals will sometimes try to disguise their handwriting in an effort to hide their crimes. Still, the examination of handwriting characteristics—when done by competent document examiners—can usually determine the origin or authenticity of the writing in question.

Ultimately, it is impossible to determine with absolute certainty that a document was written by a specific person. Handwriting analysts can offer their expert opinions, but to do so, they must have access to as many documents as possible to determine the suspect's natural style of writing. If a document examiner must present her expert opinion in court, she must honestly convey her findings, even if they are inconclusive.

The Court System and the Role of the Document Examiner

The court system in the United States brings two opposing parties together—the prosecution and the defense—to argue their case before a judge and sometimes before a jury. The nature of court is adversarial, meaning that two opposing sides attempt to win their case by presenting evidence that supports their argument. This can put the forensic scientist in a difficult position when he is called into the courtroom to testify. Each side in court is likely to bring in experts on their behalf. When questioned, document examiners are called into court to present their findings either on behalf of the prosecution or the defense; they assume the role of expert witness. In turn, their testimony will likely be questioned during cross-examination—when the attorneys on the other side have the chance to ask them questions—and may be refuted by other document examiners testifying for the other side.

Each expert can expect to be qualified before the judge and jury, which means that opposing attorneys will have the chance to ask questions about the expert's training, credentials, education, experience, and so forth. The judge sometimes has the power to disqualify any witness who does not meet certain standards for training or have proper credentials.

It is the ethical duty of the questioned document examiner to present her findings in an unbiased way. She should not act as an advocate for the side that hired her, but as an advocate for the truth and for justice. Ultimately, what she offers the judge and jury are her professional opinions rather than absolute fact. Still, opinions should be based on the scientific study of the documents involved in the case. The questioned document examiner also needs to present his or her findings in a manner that the judge and jury can understand.

Problems abound for handwriting experts when insufficient writing samples are available. If there are not enough writing samples, if the samples are altered or disguised, or if there is a lack of identifying characteristics in the handwriting, tracing the writing back to the person who wrote it proves much more difficult.

In order to help law enforcement officials collect writing samples from suspects, the FBI recommends that officers collect samples that contain matching words and phrases to the documents in question. For example, if the person is accused of forging checks, he or she should be required to write the signature that appears on the check several times to help investigators determine the suspect's natural style of writing. Whatever the suspect is accused of, law enforcement officials can require the suspect to write words that are the same or similar to those in the questioned document.

Document Examiners

Forensic document examiners can play a powerful role in helping determine the innocence or guilt of suspected criminals. Document examiners help law enforcement officers and lawyers with criminal investigations by examining evidence, writing official statements, and offering their expert opinions in criminal trials. Because of this great responsibility, they must go through special training in order to become certified.

Experts in document analysis often choose to become certified through the American Board of Forensic Document Examiners (ABFDE), which is the only certifying board sponsored and recognized by forensic organiza-

Along with being specially trained in the field, a document examiner must be ethical.

Since the late 1980s, the findings of document analysis have been recognized as scientific evidence in court cases.

tions such as the American Academy of Forensic Sciences, the American Society of Questioned Document Examiners, and the Canadian Society of Forensic Sciences. Membership in any one of these organizations helps ensure that the document examiner is professional, **ethical**, and has had specialized training in document analysis.

The minimum requirement established by the ABFDE for training in forensic document examination is a baccalaureate degree as well as a two-year, full-time **apprenticeship** in a recognized forensic laboratory or with an examiner in private practice who has previously received proper training. Certified forensic document examiners are given the title "Diplomate" by the ABFDE.

Although no federal licensing exists for forensic document examiners, the ABFDE was established in 1977 with a grant from the **U.S. Department of Justice**. The goal of the ABFDE was to recognize qualified docu-

ment examiners in government laboratories and private practice and to promote the advancement of forensic science. In 1987, a U.S. district court recognized the *legitimacy* of the ABFDE as a certifying body for forensic document examiners by denying a motion that claimed handwriting comparisons were unreliable. By referring to evidence provided by the ABFDE, the court was satisfied "that professional scientific knowledge in the subject area exists and is sufficiently reliable to be of assistance to the jury."

Over time, many different court cases have recognized that handwriting is unique enough for scientists to be able to trace the handwriting back to a particular person, as in Peter Weinberger's case. It took the special agents on the case several weeks of searching public and government records to

Like fingerprints, handwriting is considered unique to each person.

Fast Facts

Peter Weinberger's case helped pass a law allowing the FBI to enter kidnapping cases after a twenty-four-hour waiting period instead of seven days. Later, Congress signed into law the Protection of Children from Sexual Predators Act of 1998, with one provision of the law giving federal officials the authority to enter a kidnapping investigation even before the twenty-four-hour waiting period ended. With kidnappings, every minute counts.

find a handwriting sample that matched the ones in the ransom notes, but they did it. Fortunately for them, handwriting analysis had already become a scientific process, thanks to early document examiners.

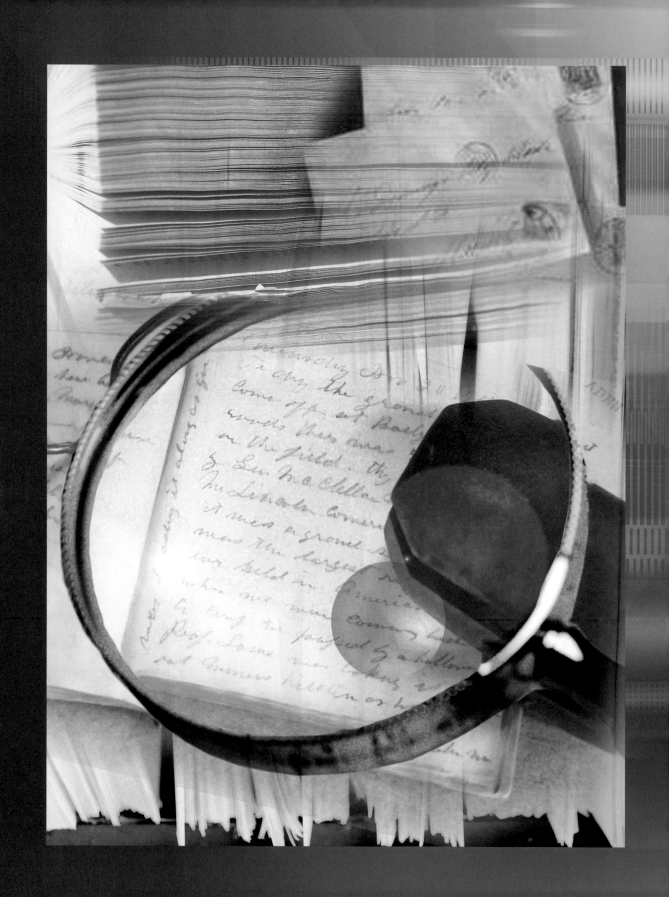

HISTORY OF THE EXAMINATION OF QUESTIONED DOCUMENTS

The first time that handwriting played a crucial role in a famous case was during what is known as the Dreyfus Affair in France in 1894–1895. The French army suspected Alfred Dreyfus, a captain in the army, of providing secret information to the German government. An army officer had found handwritten papers in a wastebasket that showed someone was giving away secrets. Although Dreyfus had access to the type of information that had been supplied to the Germans, he may have been singled out because he was Jewish; at that time, *anti-Semitism* was rampant within the French army. In any case, the army authorities declared that Dreyfus' handwriting was similar to that on the papers.

Alphonse Bertillon

Although Alphonse Bertillon lacked experience in handwriting analysis, he is credited with creating a groundbreaking identification system for criminals. In 1883, in Paris, France, before fingerprinting was discovered as a means to identify criminals, Bertillon devised a system of identification known as anthropometry. In his police work, he knew that often criminals would use aliases—phony names—to cover up the fact that they were repeat offenders, but there had been no reliable method for detecting whether the criminal was using his real name or if he was wanted for other crimes.

Bertillon had always been fascinated with the scientific method, which was a relatively new theory in the late 1800s. His father was a physician and his grandfather had been a renowned naturalist and mathematician, so Bertillon had been exposed to many scientific theories in his youth, one of them being that no two people with identical physical measurements could ever be found. He had watched his father and grandfather measure every person who came to their home. Using eleven different measurements, such as the distance between the eyes, the length of the left foot, and the width of the head, Bertillon's father and grandfather found that no two people they had ever met had the same exact physical measurements.

Bertillon later used this type of measurement on criminals, keeping the meticulously recorded information on index cards so the police could compare individuals. If two persons' measurements

matched exactly, police knew they had a repeat offender, even if the criminal gave a different name! After this was proven to be a success in the Paris police headquarters, Bertillon went on to devise other systems for keeping track of criminals, including what we now know as the "mug shot." Bertillon became known far and wide as the first man to successfully apply the scientific method to criminology.

Despite Dreyfus' declarations of innocence, he was found guilty of **treason** in a secret military court-martial, during which he was denied the right to examine the evidence against him. The army stripped him of his rank, sentenced him to life imprisonment, and shipped him off to Devil's Island, a **penal** colony located off the coast of South America.

Dreyfus' alleged espionage brought up important questions regarding the examination of handwriting in criminal trials. Unfortunately, a famous **criminalist** at the time, Alphonse Bertillon, testified against Dreyfus and helped convict him, even though Bertillon lacked expertise in handwriting comparison.

In 1906, after twelve years of national controversy and twelve years of sitting in jail, Dreyfus was exonerated of the charges and restored to his former military rank. An army officer had finally succeeded in reopening the case in light of new evidence that another officer had in fact forged the documents that led to Dreyfus' arrest and conviction. Alfred Dreyfus was free.

Standardizing Questioned Document Examination

The Dreyfus Affair brought to light the complications in handwriting examination—namely, the ethical considerations of the accusers. As discussed in chapter 1, handwriting analysis is not foolproof; unfortunately, it can be used to frame innocent people. Still, the science of studying the unique characteristics in penmanship has grown over the years.

Handwriting contains many clues.

Court Cases That Set Scientific Standards

In 1923, the District of Columbia Circuit Court addressed whether the results of a polygraph examination (lie detector test) were admissible evidence in the case Frye v. United States. The decision set what is now known as the "Frye Standard" for presenting scientific evidence in court. The standard states that the court can accept expert testimony on "well-recognized scientific principle and discovery" if it is "sufficiently established" and has achieved "general acceptance" in the scientific community.

Though the Frye Standard was in place for many years and is still used in many jurisdictions, it has been replaced more recently by Daubert v. Merrell Dow Pharmaceutical, Inc., or Rule 702 of the Federal Rules of Evidence. Rule 702 states that judges may use their discretion to admit expert testimony to "understand the evidence" and to "determine a fact in issue." Rule 702 was upheld in 1993 by the U.S. Supreme Court, which held that the "general acceptance" clause in Frye was not absolute, thereby granting judges more discretion as to what expert testimony they may allow in court.

In an effort to rid the courtroom of "junk science," the high Court laid out guidelines to help judges decide which expert testimony to allow. In order for a new scientific technique or theory to be acceptable to a court, it must be spelled out, tested, reviewed, accepted by the scientific community, and continually monitored for accuracy. If the theory or technique meets the Frye or Daubert standards, the judge allows the jury to hear the expert testimony; if not, the judge has the discretion to exclude it from the trial.

In the eastern United States, around the same time as the Dreyfus Affair, the standardization of the science of questioned document examination was under way. In the late 1800s, two examiners, William E. Hagan and Persifor Frazer, each published a book, Hagan's Disputed Handwriting and Frazer's *A Manual for the Study of Documents*. According to Joe Nickell and Jon F. Fischer in *Crime Science: Methods of Forensic Detection*, Hagan's book was "the first significant modern text that attempted a thoroughly scientific approach to questioned documents."

In 1900, Daniel T. Ames, another document examiner, published *Ames on Forgery*. All three books offered insight into the complicated realm of

Dear Sir:
Please send me the following items at your

Dear Sir:
PLEASE SEND ME THE FOLLOWING ITEMS AT YOUR EARLIEST

Dear Sir:
Please send me the following items at you

Dear Sir:
Please send me the following items at your Earliest

Each person's penmanship has unique characteristics.

Women in the Field

All early workers in the field of questioned document examination were men. In the 1930s, a few women entered the profession. In 1931, Katherine Applegate Keeler served as staff document examiner at the Scientific Crime Detection Laboratory in Chicago. Elizabeth McCarthy worked in Boston and testified for the first time in 1934, and Mary Beacom of Atlanta started work as a questioned document examiner in 1937.

questioned document examination. In 1910, however, the most comprehensive text on the subject was published: Albert S. Osborn's book *Questioned Documents*. According to Ordway Hilton, a renowned document examiner of the twentieth century, "The scope and treatment of the subject [in Osborn's book] completely overshadowed the work of the three previous writers."

What set Osborn apart from the other published document examiners was that he was concerned with all aspects of questioned document work, from methods of examination to the newest techniques, and from court presentation to the legal decisions affecting document examination. In 1922, he published a second book, *The Problem of Proof*, in which he discussed courtroom procedure and advocated for more liberal legal rules concerning expert testimony of questioned document examiners.

Osborn set the standards for the examination of questioned documents. His first book, which was revised in 1929, continues to be used today as a reference for all questioned document examiners. Through Osborn's efforts, scientific evidence involving disputed documents was first accepted by courts in the United States.

In 1914, Osborn organized an informal gathering of a few questioned document examiners in New York to discuss aspects of their work. Every summer thereafter the invitation was renewed to a few select questioned document examiners. They shared a willingness to participate in a mutual education program and to discuss problems in the field of questioned document examination. The circle grew throughout the 1920s and 1930s until they became officially organized as the American Society of Questioned Document Examiners in 1942.

Osborn and his colleagues made much progress in questioned document work during those decades. Typewriting identification improved, the first paper on the use of ultraviolet light was published, new methods for restoring erased ink were developed, infrared photography was applied to document examination for the first time, handwriting examination improved, and the groundwork for deciphering charred documents was formed. Basically, the principles of handwriting identification and detecting forgery were standardized, and the work of skilled questioned document examiners was shown to be a scientific procedure.

In 1977, The American Board of Forensic Document Examiners was organized. Later, the Board of Forensic Document Examiners was also founded. These two organizations are the only certifying boards of questioned document examiners in the United States and Canada. Membership in these organizations means that the examiner has completed formal education and training in questioned document work.

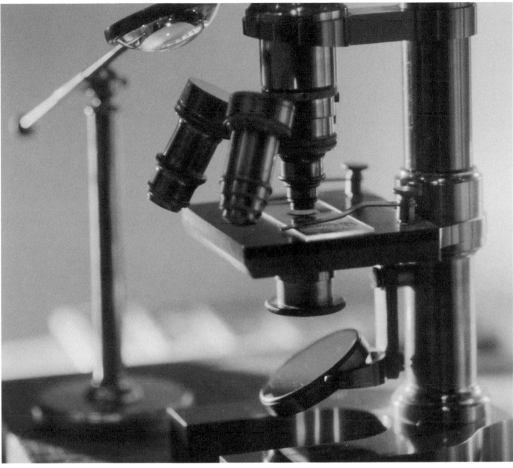

Microscopes and other scientific tools can help detect forgeries.

The First Crime Laboratories

Until the 1920s, private examiners did all the work of questioned document examiners. The organization of the Scientific Crime Detection Laboratory in Chicago, the first forensic science laboratory, began in 1929. Professor John H. Wigmore of Northwestern University School of Law, one of the men who used to meet yearly with Albert S. Osborn, was the driving force behind the creation of the lab. It started under private endowment, but within a couple of years it became affiliated with Northwestern University and in 1938 became a unit of the Chicago Police Department.

This first lab offered expert information on the science of questioned documents, and helped educate the federal government's crime science technicians, who were working simultaneously to establish the first FBI Crime Laboratory.

Today's FBI Crime Laboratory handles all types of forensic analysis, including the study of fingerprints.

Soon after the creation of the Chicago Crime Lab, the U.S. government opened the first federal crime lab at the United States Bureau of Investigations (the name was changed to the Federal Bureau of Investigations in 1935). At the time, there was only one special agent, Charles Appel. He helped to pioneer the laboratory and was in charge of getting it off the ground.

Appel became trained in handwriting and typewriter analysis and other areas of forensic science through the Scientific Crime Detection Lab. Over time, he persuaded the FBI to open its own crime lab. Appel believed that eventually the FBI would become a clearinghouse of information and that police departments from all over the country would look to the FBI for information and support.

The official date that the FBI Crime Lab opened is considered November 24, 1932, although it was set in motion in the mid-1920s. J. Edgar Hoover, the director of the bureau starting in 1924, was captivated by scientific crime detection, and he encouraged the bureau to keep up to date with the latest available technology. Hoover was the main supporter of Appel's work in forensic science, particularly in the examination of questioned documents, and Hoover encouraged Appel's further training in the field.

When the new FBI Crime Lab opened in Room 802 of the Old Southern Railway Building at Thirteenth Street and Pennsylvania Avenue in Washington, D.C., Appel set it up with the most advanced scientific equipment of the time, including a new ultraviolet light machine and a microscope on loan from the Bausch & Lomb company.

During the first few months, important bureau policy was set to ensure control of evidence coming into the bureau and restricting the number of persons involved in handling it. As the only lab technician, Appel was lim-

ited in how many cases he could help solve, though with the hired help of outside sources, he managed to perform more than one thousand examinations in the first year alone, as well as publish research papers. In 1935, two more special agents were assigned to assist Appel in the lab.

The FBI Crime Lab Today

In 2002, the FBI Crime Lab moved into a new, state-of-the-art building in Quantico, Virginia. The lab is involved in every kind of forensic analysis, from the study of firearms, questioned documents, and **latent fingerprints**, to scientific analysis involving chemistry, DNA analysis, explosive devices, and microscopic trace evidence such as hairs and fibers. The crime lab focuses on research and development of new technologies in forensic science.

The Questioned Documents Unit (QDU) of the crime lab examines and compares data appearing on paper and other materials. These surface data include handwriting, hand printing, typewriting, printing, erasures, alterations, and obliterations. Impressions such as those from indented writing or use of a check writer or dry seal in the surface of paper are also examined. (Such impressions will be discussed further in chapters 4 and 5.)

Additionally, data such as watermarks, safety fibers, and other integral features within paper or other surfaces may also be components of document examinations. The QDU maintains a number of databases—the Anonymous Letter File, the Bank Robbery Note File, the National Fraudulent Check File, the Watermark File, and the Shoeprint File—to assist forensic scientists in their investigations.

Fast Facts

The FBI Crime Lab has come a long way from a one-man operation. Today, over 500 special agents and experts work at the lab.

With over eighty years of experience in the study of forensic science, the FBI Crime Lab is a leading source for solving crimes. It has indeed realized the dream of Charles Appel.

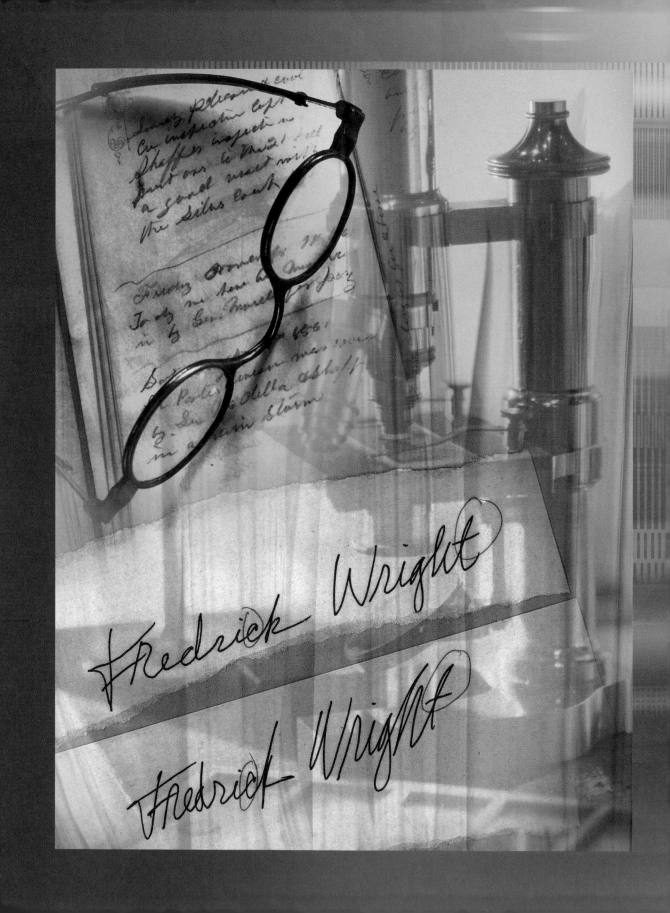

3

HANDWRITING COMPARISON: THE CRIME OF THE CENTURY

Charles Appel and Albert S. Osborn both became involved in one of the most famous cases of the twentieth century: the kidnapping of Charles A. Lindbergh's son, twenty-month-old Charles Jr. Lindbergh Sr. was a famous *aviator*, the first pilot to fly solo across the Atlantic Ocean. He was also very wealthy, which made his family a target for kidnapping.

On the night of March 1, 1932, Lindbergh and his wife, the poet Anne Morrow Lindbergh, put Charles Jr. to bed in their home just outside Hopewell, New Jersey. At nine o'clock that evening, Mrs. Lindbergh checked on her son and found him sleeping peacefully in his bed. Fifty minutes later, the baby's nurse found him missing.

When police arrived a short while later, they discovered a handwritten ransom note on the nursery's windowsill. It demanded fifty thousand dollars for return of the boy. The note said:

Dear Sir!
Have 50000$ redy with 2500$ in 20$ bills 1500$ in 10$ bills and 1000$ in 5$ bills. After 2-4 days we will inform you were to deliver the Mony. We warn you for making anyding public or for notify the polise the child is in gute care.
Indication for all letters are singnature and 3 holes.

At the bottom right-hand corner of the note was a drawing of two interlocking circles. The area where the circles intersected had been colored red and three small holes had been punched into the design. This design would appear on all the notes from the kidnapper to identify them as genuine.

Based on the handwriting and grammar, detectives believed the kidnapper was probably of German descent, but had been in America for at least a few years. Furthermore, because the kidnapper used a homemade ladder to climb into the second-floor nursery window, they guessed he was a carpenter. Further evidence pointed to the kidnapper as someone living in the Bronx.

On March 6, a second ransom note was delivered, admonishing Charles Lindbergh for getting the police involved and increasing the ransom demand to $70,000. Two days after that, the third ransom note was delivered to Lindbergh's attorney, asking for an intermediary to negotiate payment of the ransom money. On the same day, Dr. John F. Condon published a note in the Bronx Home News offering to act as a go-between and offering another $1,000 in ransom money.

In the infamous Lindbergh case, negotiations were arranged first through handwritten ransom notes and then newspaper columns.

The next day, Dr. Condon received the fourth ransom note, indicating that he would be acceptable as an intermediary. Lindbergh also accepted this, and on March 10, Dr. Condon received $70,000 in ransom money and began negotiations for payment through newspaper columns under the code name "Jafsic." Part of the ransom money was administered in gold certificates, which was currency based on the gold standard. The government would recall all gold certificates the following year.

On March 12, Dr. Condon received the fifth ransom note delivered by a taxicab driver who said he received it from an unidentified stranger. The message said that there would be another note under a stone at a vacant stand near a subway station. Dr. Condon found the note, followed the instructions on it, and went to meet a man who called himself "John" at the Woodlawn Cemetery. They discussed payment of the ransom money, and

Kidnappers claimed the Lindbergh baby was being held on a boat such as this one near Martha's Vineyard.

Dr. Condon tried to get more information out of "John" as to the where-abouts of the baby. "John" said to Dr. Condon, "Will I burn if the baby's dead?"

"Is the baby dead?" asked Dr. Condon.

"John" reassured him the baby was alive and offered to send the baby's sleeping suit as a token of the child's identity.

Over the next few days, Dr. Condon repeated his advertisements in the newspaper, urging further contact and stating his willingness to pay the ransom. On March 16, Charles Lindbergh received the baby's pajamas along with the seventh ransom note. The eighth ransom note was received

by Dr. Condon on March 21, insisting complete compliance with his demands. These notes and demands continued over the next week and a half.

In all, thirteen ransom notes were delivered either to the Lindberghs or Dr. Condon as they tried to negotiate payment of the ransom and return of the boy. Finally, on April 2, more than one month after the kidnapping, Condon again met with "John" to deliver the ransom money in exchange for a receipt and a note claiming that the baby was held on a boat off the coast of Martha's Vineyard. Lindbergh spent two fruitless days searching for his son before returning to New Jersey empty-handed.

On May 12, more than two months after the kidnapping, the body of Charles Jr. was found accidentally about 4.5 miles (7.2 kilometers) from the Lindbergh home. Charles Lindbergh positively identified the remains of his son, and the baby was cremated the next day. More than a year passed before the kidnapper, Bruno Richard Hauptmann, was caught when he spent one of the gold certificates from the ransom money at a gas station. The attendant found this suspicious and wrote down Hauptmann's license plate number.

Hauptmann's handwriting played a pivotal role in his guilty verdict. Several handwriting experts all agreed that the same person wrote all the ransom notes. The kidnapper signed them with the same symbol, and they often contained the same misspellings and grammatical errors, such as "mony" for "money" and "houers" for "hours." Also, all notes had an odd inversion of certain letters, such as "g" and "h." They had all been written on the same kind of paper with the same ink.

Some people, however, dispute whether it really was Hauptmann who wrote the ransom notes. He proclaimed his innocence throughout the trial and said the ransom money found in his home was given to him by Isador Fisch, a man who had left the United States to return to Germany, where he had died. According to Katherine Ramsland in the article "Literary Foren-

sics," Hauptmann was required to give writing samples over and over until he was exhausted and fell asleep at the table. He was instructed to write the notes using different paper and inks, at different angles, and many times in order for document examiners to get a sense of his natural style, as it was assumed that Hauptmann would try to disguise his earliest writing samples.

Originally, Investigator Albert D. Osborn (the son of Albert S. Osborn) didn't believe that Hauptmann was the writer of the ransom notes. So the police demanded more writing samples. Hauptmann was even told to copy photostats of the ransom notes, which is improper protocol at best, and unethical at worst. Albert S. and Albert D. Osborn remained unconvinced that Hauptmann was the writer of the ransom notes; however, when told that he had possession of much of the ransom money, they changed their minds and testified that Hauptmann had written them.

Hauptmann may have successfully disguised his handwriting, either when giving the court his required samples or when writing the ransom notes. Other evidence pointed to his guilt. Besides possession of much of the ransom money, Hauptmann was positively identified by Dr. Condon as the man who claimed to be "John." There seemed to be little evidence pointing to Hauptmann's innocence.

Bruno Richard Hauptmann was found guilty of kidnapping and murder, and was executed in the electric chair on April 3, 1936. His handwriting helped kill him.

What's So Special About Handwriting?

No two people write exactly alike, not even identical twins. When we learn to write, we copy big block letters. Our focus is on imitating what is pre-

Experts maintain that our handwriting changes as we grow older.

sented to us, rather than the content of what we are writing. Only after learning how to write script (cursive) and after years of practice, do we take on unique penmanship qualities. Our writing becomes unconscious as we focus less on shaping lines and curves and more on meaning. By the time we reach our late teens, our writing style is as ingrained as the way we talk.

Still, over time our handwriting undergoes gradual changes that are not very dramatic but are recognizable. When handwriting experts need to examine two handwriting samples, they will do better if they have known samples of the suspect's handwriting written within twenty years of the

The "Other" Handwriting Analysis: Graphology

Handwriting may contain many clues about a person's educational or ethnic background, but it does not—according to forensic scientists—reveal someone's personality. However, the individuality of handwriting does serve as the basis for a type of "handwriting analysis" called graphology. Graphology tries to predict someone's character or personality traits from their handwriting.

Graphology, however, is not considered a real science, and therefore is not acceptable in a court of law. Forensic science is based on the assumption that there is a real knowable world that operates according to fixed rules and can be revealed through direct observation. In order to be accepted by the courts, evidence presented by forensic document examiners must be based on sound scientific principles and subject to the scientific method, as discussed in chapter 1. Graphology is not considered a real science because it has little, if any, experimental foundation.

Still, many people fervently believe in the worth of graphology, with the principle behind it being that people who share certain character and personality traits also exhibit similar shapes and forms in their handwriting. The International Graphoanalysis Society (IGAS) trains thousands of people annually in the field. In order to belong to IGAS, a grapho-analyst must abide by a strict code of ethics, including the acknowledgment that training in graphology does not certify someone in questioned document examination.

document in question. If more time has passed between the two writing samples, there's a chance that handwriting even by the same person will look different.

We also never write the same way twice. Your signature will never look exactly the same way no matter how many times you write it. You can try this by writing your name ten times on a piece of paper. This fact is the bane of document examiners. If the document in question is something with a signature on it, like a simple forged check, document examiners can usually tell it's been forged if the signature matches almost exactly an authentic signature. On the other hand, one person's handwriting may look radically different depending on what type of instrument she used (pen, pencil, marker) and whether she wrote with the paper on a table or up against the wall. Furthermore, stress, illness, disability, or inebriation can also affect a person's handwriting. Document examiners must keep these variables in mind when examining questioned documents.

Obtaining Standards for Comparison

Ideally, document examiners will obtain several writing samples—called standards—to get a feel for the person's natural style of writing. Preferably, the standards they obtain would be nonrequested standards, meaning they did not have to ask the suspect to write anything, and the samples are known to be the person's authentic handwriting. If no known nonrequested standards are available, the examiner may ask the suspected writer to produce several writing samples; these are known as requested standards.

The advantage to acquiring nonrequested standards is that the writing reveals the true nature of the suspected writer's handwriting. The writing style will be his natural style, and the documents may also reveal common words or phrases the writer normally uses. For example, old letters or diaries may contain words or phrases unique to the ones in a ransom note. The problem with nonrequested standards is that they must be authenticated. If no one can trace the samples back to the suspected writer, they cannot be used as evidence.

Of course, when obtaining standards for comparison, document examiners must be absolutely certain they are authentic. In the next chapter, we'll examine a famous forgery of Adolf Hitler's diaries. At first they were believed to be authentic because the handwriting in the diaries matched

Diaries are an example of handwritten documents that can be forged.

Hitler's handwriting that had been kept in the German Federal Archives. Unfortunately, Hitler's "handwriting samples" were actually earlier forged works of the man who forged the diaries!

With requested standards, no one questions their authenticity. For example, in the case of Bruno Richard Hauptmann, authenticating his writing samples wasn't necessary, since they were requested samples. The risk with requested samples is that a suspect may intentionally attempt to disguise her normal handwriting.

The legality of requiring suspects to provide handwriting samples was established in 1967 in *Gilbert v. California*. The U.S. Supreme Court ruled that requiring a suspect to submit handwriting samples before the court is legal and does not violate protection under the Fifth Amendment, which allows a suspect the right not to incriminate or testify against himself. In 1973, the Court also decided that requiring suspects to submit handwriting samples doesn't violate the Fourth Amendment's protections against unreasonable search and seizure. So any court in the United States can order a suspect to provide handwriting samples even if he refuses.

The FBI has set standards for obtaining writing samples. The investigators should sit the suspect at a table where there will be no distractions, and an objective witness should observe the procedure as follows:

- The suspect should not be shown the questioned document.
- The suspect should not be told how to spell certain words or to use certain punctuation.
- The suspect should use materials similar to those of the document.
- The dictated text should match some parts of the document.
- The dictation should be repeated at least three times.
- The suspect should be asked to sign the text.

Handwriting Comparision   **47**

What Do Handwriting Experts Look For?

One of the first questions document examiners attempt to answer is whether the handwriting is in the suspect's natural style. Often when someone forges a long document, she stops to check for spelling and punctuation so frequently that the writing in the document contains numerous places where the writer obviously lifted the pen from the paper. Also, when a criminal writes a ransom or bank robbery note, he may deliberately try to disguise his handwriting. For example, obvious spelling and grammar mistakes can suggest that the writer was deliberately disguising his mastery of the English language. Likewise, numerous inconsistencies in the flow of the script suggest that the writing is not in the person's normal writing style.

Document examiners also look for individual characteristics in handwriting as opposed to class characteristics. For example, the handwriting style students learn in a particular script copybook yields class characteristics; in other words, the writing style belongs to a particular group. The style that students develop over time doesn't belong to any such group. Each person's unique handwriting style contains individual characteristics. For example, in most cases, a standard script "a" in handwriting copybooks is closed at the top, and the final downstroke retraces the upstroke; those are class characteristics. The way one person writes an "a" may be open at the top or have a little curl at the bottom. Those are individual characteristics.

How forensic document examiners check out individual characteristics can be grouped into these categories:

- **Overall form** refers to a number of characteristics that shape the elements in the handwriting, such as the size, shape, slant, proportion, and the beginning and ending strokes of the letters.

- **Line features** refer to the speed and fluidity of the handwriting, the amount of pressure used in the writing, the spacing between letters and words, and how the letters are connected. The type of writing instrument used may influence these characteristics. For example, a flexible-point pen produces lines that are more expressive and revealing of a writer's habits than a ballpoint pen or a pencil.

Alcohol can influence handwriting.

Handwriting Comparision

Ballpoint Pens Changed Handwriting Analysis

On October 30, 1945, the Reynolds ballpoint pen was first sold at Gimbels in New York City. The new pen and its copies took the country by storm; within a year the price of the pen had dropped dramatically, and ballpoint pens were sold by the thousands. Within ten years, the ballpoint pen was the most popular writing instrument, replacing fountain pens as the North American number-one choice.

Ballpoint pens presented new challenges to document examiners. The manufacturing technique and the quality of the inks involved led to patchy results that document examiners couldn't always tell from pen lifts or pauses that might indicate forgeries. Examiners had to learn how to differentiate between faults of forgery and defects of the typical ballpoint pen.

In 1975, the first roller ballpoint pen was introduced with fluid, water-based ink that offered a smoother flow. Then, in 1979, PaperMate introduced the first erasable pen. When fresh, its ink could be easily erased, creating yet another challenge for document examiners.

Nowadays, the average North American can choose from dozens of different kinds of pens and several types of inks. For document examiners, it's important to keep up with changes in manufacture, design, and technology in order to better analyze handwriting.

- **Arrangement** includes how the writing is presented on the page. For example, the width of the margins and the consistency of the spacing give some clues as to how the suspect normally writes. The slanting between lines also shows consistencies.
- **Content** refers to grammar, punctuation, spelling, and word choice, which can help point out consistent errors, repeated phrases, and other clues that can hint at a writer's ethnicity or educational level.

Document examiners look at all these features to help them determine whether a suspect's handwriting and the questioned writing match. Based on the findings, the examiner may come to one of four conclusions: the handwriting absolutely matches, the handwriting matches with a high probability, the handwriting probably matches, the handwriting does not match.

Not every examination leads to a conclusive finding. In rare cases, the examiner may say she can't make a determination based on the writing samples.

At Bruno Richard Hauptmann's trial, the prosecution brought in several handwriting experts who all testified that Hauptmann wrote the ransom notes. Hauptmann's attorney, Edward J. Reilly, claimed he would have just as many handwriting experts counter this testimony, but in fact, he presented only two weak "experts." Most handwriting experts he had originally contacted refused to testify in Hauptmann's defense, likely because the handwriting was such a close match that it would have been unethical to claim otherwise. At the end of his trial, one of the few things Hauptmann said was, "Dat handwriting is the worstest thing against me."

That may have been true for Hauptmann—but others have managed to fool handwriting experts with their forgeries, if only for a little while.

FORGERY DETECTION: UNCOVERING ADOLF HITLER'S "DIARIES"

4

In 1983, a popular West German magazine, *Stern*, declared to the world that they had possession of sixty-two volumes of Adolf Hitler's diaries. The diaries were entirely handwritten and allegedly had been rescued from a downed Nazi plane that had crashed and burned in April 1945. The documents reportedly survived the fire because they were protected in a metal-lined container.

Two years earlier, when *Stern* had first gotten hold of some of the volumes, they set about authenticating them by sending samples of the diaries to handwriting experts Dr. Max Frei-Sulzer of Switzerland and Ordway Hilton of the United States. Along with the diaries, they sent examples of Hitler's handwriting gathered from the German Federal Archives. The handwriting experts pro-

claimed the handwriting in the diaries was a match to the handwriting of Hitler, and therefore declared the diaries authentic. What they didn't know was that the handwriting samples were not written by Adolf Hitler but by the man who forged the diaries, an East German named Konrad Kujau.

According to Rachael Bell in *Hitler's Diaries*, Konrad Kujau was a Hitler enthusiast ever since he had been a little boy in the early 1940s. His father died when he was six years old, and his mother became so poor that she often sent him and his sisters to live in various orphanages. Kujau was a bright student and an eager learner who became adept at painting and art. He often painted pictures of his hero, Adolf Hitler. After he left school as a

Nazi memorabilia, like that which Kujau collected.

teenager, he worked a series of jobs, including locksmith, window washer, and waiter, but none of the positions lasted long. In 1957, he moved from East Germany to the suburbs of Stuttgart, West Germany, and began a life of petty crime. Over the years he was arrested for such charges as theft, burglary, and fighting in public.

His first-known forgery was counterfeiting lunch vouchers in exchange for a small profit. He was caught, arrested, and sentenced to a short time in jail. Around the same time, he began a relationship with a woman named Edith Leiblang, and together they started a cleaning company, which didn't make a profit in the way they'd hoped. In the aftermath of this failed business venture, Kujau began collecting Nazi memorabilia and quickly learned that there was a large market for relics from that era. By the mid-1970s, Kujau was considered to be one of the largest collectors of Third Reich artifacts in West Germany, and he established a store in which to display and sell his many items.

It didn't take Kujau long to learn that he could double and even triple his profit by forging some of the artifacts with signatures of once-prominent Nazis. Using his creativity and talent, he even created bogus authentication documents to accompany the forged artifacts. Some of the relics he sold included Nazi helmets, flags, uniforms, medals, and documents allegedly written by former **SS officials**. Eventually, he began forging Hitler's signature . . . which made him very rich.

Surprisingly, the majority of buyers never questioned the authenticity of the artifacts and documents or how Kujau came to have them in his possession. Kujau would even invent stories about them to make them more compelling to his buyers. Thus he became a spectacular salesman and successful dealer in Nazi memorabilia.

Buoyed by his successes, Kujau became increasingly bold, and by the late 1970s, he had decided to take on an even more elaborate project. He

Most of us are fascinated by historical diaries—and Kujau took advantage of this fact.

forged two copies of Adolf Hitler's Mein Kampf, which means "My Struggle" and is Hitler's autobiographical account of his resistance against the German establishment and his incarceration in the 1920s. Kujau produced two handwritten volumes as well as a preface to a third book. While the two volumes of Mein Kampf were forgeries (as the book really does exist), the preface to the third book was completely fabricated from Kujau's imagination.

Kujau continued to forge works in Hitler's name, including poems allegedly written by Hitler that were quickly sold off to wealthy buyers. Soon thereafter, Kujau began crafting the sixty-two volumes of the Hitler diaries that would eventually come into the possession of *Stern* magazine.

In the fall of 1979, another Hitler enthusiast, Gerd Hiedemann, viewed several of the forged diaries in the home of an acquaintance named Fritz Steifel. Hiedemann, who worked as an investigative reporter for *Stern*, was completely dazzled by the diaries. He did some research and learned about the plane crash and the mysterious cache of papers. He also learned that there were reportedly twenty-seven or more volumes of the "lost" diaries in possession of a man named Konrad Fischer, who was really Konrad Kujau. Konrad Fischer was one of several of Kujau's aliases.

Based on the information Hiedemann uncovered, he was able to convince his employers at Stern to make an offer to purchase twenty-seven volumes of the Hitler diaries. However, it was difficult for Hiedemann to locate Kujau, in part because of his use of aliases and in part because Kujau feared that increased publicity would expose him as a fraud. However, Kujau could not resist the money. *Stern* had offered to pay approximately 2 million marks for the diaries, which Kujau accepted, and then set about to produce the volumes as quickly as possible.

Finally, in January 1981, Kujau presented one of the diaries to Hiedemann, who then turned it over to Stern's parent company, Gruner and Jahr, who had helped finance the purchase. Apparently, the excitement surrounding the deal skewed the judgment of those involved, for amazingly, no one had yet bothered to authenticate the diary.

Over time, *Stern*'s publishers decided to auction off the diaries to the highest bidder. In an attempt to authenticate them, they sent copies of the diaries along with copies of Hitler's alleged true handwriting to the handwriting experts mentioned earlier in this chapter. Kujau had been such a clever scam artist, however, that the samples of Hitler's alleged handwriting held in the German Federal Archives were actually the forged works Kujau

Fast Facts

Two million German marks would be worth about $1,360,405,966.36 in today's U.S. dollars and about $1,335,795,755.95 in Canadian dollars. However, German marks are now obsolete, having been replaced by the euro in 2002.

had completed earlier. Therefore, the handwriting samples matched, and the documents were declared authentic.

Fibers and Fillers: What to Check When Handwriting Matches

So how were the diaries revealed as fakes when the handwriting in the diaries matched the handwriting in Hitler's "real" documents?

The first clue that the diaries weren't real came from outraged citizens and historians who challenged the authenticity of the diaries based on the fact that they didn't seem to be written in Hitler's true "voice." In other words, the diaries presented Hitler as much more likable and nicer than historical and eyewitness accounts reveal. The diaries horrified people who had firsthand experience of some of Hitler's atrocities in his infamous concentration camps.

In order to set the record straight, *Stern* and Gruner and Jahr agreed to let the diaries undergo more rigorous testing. West Germany's Federal

Archives ran a series of tests on the diaries. Forensic scientists chemically tested several of the volumes to find out if the paper, glue, ink, and bindings were from the period during Hitler's reign. What they discovered shocked the publishing world: the tests revealed that the paper, ink, and glue were undoubtedly manufactured post–World War II. The paper contained *blankophor*, a whitener that didn't exist until 1954. The bindings contained threads of viscose and polyester, neither of which existed in the 1940s, and the inks used in the diaries were not widely available during World War II.

The diaries were nothing but worthless forgeries.

Analyzing Papers and Inks

Document examiners have a variety of tools at their disposal to analyze the material on which something is written as well as the medium used, such as a typewriter or ink. In forgeries where there are attempts to alter a document, the paper's surface generally shows the erasure, sandpapering,

Scientists can track the age of ink in order to authenticate a document.

or razor marks that have been applied to the surface. Often, examiners can see these alterations with the naked eye, but even if they can't, they can use these tools to check:

- A magnifying glass or a microscope used with oblique (angled) lighting uncovers most erasures.
- Ultraviolet or infrared light may expose tiny fragments of eraser or ink that's been forced into the fibers of the paper, as well as any alteration made with a different color of ink.
- Lycopodium powder clings to and exposes tiny rubber particles and eraser fragments when it is dusted over the page.

As for inks, the U.S. Bureau of Alcohol, Tobacco, and Firearms keeps an ink database of more than three thousand profiles for checking and comparing inks. Modern ink can be one of four basic types: iron salts in a suspension of gallic acid, carbon particles suspended in gum arabic, synthetic dyes with a range of polymers and acids, and synthetic dyes or pigments in a range of solvents and additives.

One method of comparing questioned ink is through a process called *microspectrophotometry*. This enables the examiner to determine whether the colors of two inks in a document match by comparing their light transmission, absorption, and reflection characteristics.

Another method for comparing ink is thin-layer, which involves four steps:

1. Very small samples of the inked paper are punched from the written lines using a thin hollow needle.
2. The tiny pieces of paper are placed in a test tube, and a solvent that dissolves the ink is added.

Examiners use the scientific method to analyze ink samples.

3. A drop of the solvent solution, which now carries the ink, is placed on a paper strip along with drops of several known inks.
4. The strip is dried and then dipped into another solvent that migrates up the paper strip, dragging the inks along with it.

The distances that the inks travel along the strip are determined by the size of their molecules. This process separates the inks into bands, and whenever inks from two pages of a questioned document are tested and yield different bands, they are undoubtedly from two different ink sources.

Exposing Forgeries Through Handwriting Analysis

If the Hitler diaries had been compared to Hitler's actual handwriting, they would have immediately been exposed as fakes; although Kujau may have been able to simulate Hitler's signature, his longer forged works could not have imitated Hitler's handwriting successfully. It's nearly impossible that anyone could imitate someone else's handwriting in such lengthy works or for such an extended period of time.

Document examiners look for certain clues when investigating alleged forged works. According to Cyril H. Wecht in *Crime Scene Investigation*, telltale signs that give away forged writings include:

- evidence of previous writing, which can include underlying tracing of the words or signature

Because a person's handwriting is unique, it is impossible to convincingly forge a lengthy work.

Other Telltale Signs of Forgery

In addition to analyzing the handwriting in a suspected forgery, document examiners will also check the paper for signs that something has been changed, obliterated, or erased. These changes are all called alterations. Alterations may be as simple as changing a date on a document or changing the amount of a check so that the forger can cash it for more money, or it may be as complicated as changing portions of a document, such as a will, to benefit the forger.

For example, in the case of a will, the forger may obliterate portions of the text and then replace the obliterated text. However, whenever someone obliterates writing before making changes to the document, the examiner can usually see the changes in the underlying paper and analyze the new text by comparing it with the old. Occasionally, the forged work is so well done that the examiner cannot detect changes with the naked eye, so he will use a microscope to check for slight changes in ink color, line thickness, and pen pressure, as well as double lines or other subtle differences that may appear under the microscope.

- tremors, or shakiness, in the writing, indicated by fine yet distinguishable markings
- uneven writing and pen pressure
- hesitations
- unusual pen lifts, where the forger continually checks his or her handiwork

- patching and retouching, fixing or adding marks
- blunt beginnings and endings

Kujau managed to cover his forgeries at first by setting things up so that his earliest forged works were the ones his Hitler diaries were compared to; therefore, any telltale signs of forgery were not apparent to the handwriting analysts.

Following the Paper Trail: Watermarks and Other Giveaways

Most paper is made of wood and cotton and often contains chemical additives that affect its color, opacity, strength, brightness, and durability. These additives include:

- coatings, which improve the appearance and surface properties of the paper and may even improve the paper for use in copiers or printers
- fillers, which add color, strength, and surface texture
- sizings, which make the surface less porous to ink, so that writing and printing appear sharp and clear

The types and amounts of additives in paper vary greatly among paper manufacturers and paper types. These differences allow document examiners to distinguish one type of paper and manufacturer from another.

Another distinguishing characteristic of paper is its watermark, a translucent design that indicates the manufacturer, the date of its production,

and sometimes for whom the paper was produced. Watermarks can be seen by the naked eye simply by holding the paper up toward a light source. Forged watermarks are easy for document examiners to spot because true watermarks have fewer fibers than the rest of the page, whereas forged watermarks are added images and thus have an underlying fiber density equal to that of the rest of the paper.

Forgeries Involving Typewriters, Printers, and Photocopiers

Many criminals operate under the mistaken impression that by using a typewriter, printer, or photocopier to write threatening letters, or ransom or **extortion** notes, their writing will not be traceable. However, in the same way that humans develop individual characteristics in their handwriting,

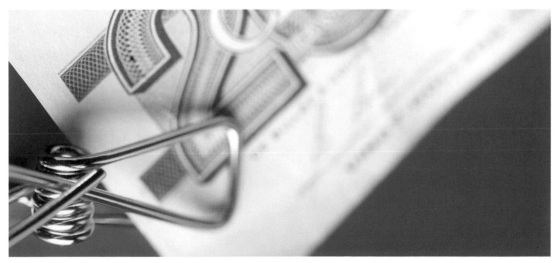

Currency has embedded watermarks that are difficult to replicate.

machines such as typewriters and photocopiers also develop individual characteristics. Because of this, documents can be traced back to the machine that produced them.

Although computer printers are much more common these days than typewriters, a surprising number of forged artifacts are still done on typewriters, and document examiners today still perform many examinations on typewritten documents. Documents printed on computer printers are much more difficult to trace than documents from typewriters because it takes longer for printers to develop individual characteristics than it does for typewriters. It is possible to trace a document back to the computer that produced it through what's known as computer forensics, but tracing a paper document back to a computer printer rarely produces definitive results.

In fact, according to F. Harley Norwitch, a questioned document examiner in Florida, it is nearly impossible to trace a document back to a printer. "In cases where a computer and printer are involved, the identification process is so remote as to be almost non-existent," he writes. "Many times, for instance, the ability to even distinguish between a laser printer and a photocopier cannot be reliably accomplished. Even though the two machines have quite different uses, their output can be essentially the same." It is much easier to differentiate between typewriters than computer printers.

When a typewritten document is involved in a crime, the document examiner will first attempt to determine the make and model of the typewriter, and then to match the note with the typewriter of a suspect, if one is available. In order to do this, document examiners access a database of typefaces used in various typewriter models, both new and old. The size, shape, and style of the letters may vary among manufacturers, making identification of the company possible. The next step is to refine the search and narrow it down to the exact machine that produced the document.

To find the exact machine that produced the document in question, examiners look for individual characteristics, such as misaligned or damaged letters, abnormal spacing before or after certain letters, and variations in the pressure applied to the page by some letters. Also, certain letters may have nicks or other defects that are imprinted on the page, or the machine itself may print to one side slightly higher or lower than the other.

Copy machines also develop distinctive traits over time. Photocopy machines duplicate images from one page onto another through a series of events. First, a lens focuses the image of the original page onto a drum that is charged with static electricity and coated with a light-sensitive substance. Then the drum is bathed with a toner powder that attaches the image to the surface of the drum. The toner image is then transferred to the blank page.

Investigators can sometimes trace a document back to a particular photocopy machine because the mechanisms within it that move the paper

Typewriters develop traits over time that link a document to the machine on which it was created.

around may leave marks on the paper. Similarly, the lens, cover glass, or drum may have scratches or defects that mark every page it produces.

Testing the machines is therefore rather simple. Document examiners can simply type or photocopy new documents to see if the individual characteristics match. Typewriters that use ribbons can help document examiners link the typewriter to a questioned document. Sometimes the ribbons used in the suspected typewriter are still in the machine when the investigator checks it; in that case, the document examiner can just read the message right off the ribbon.

A major problem can arise when a forger uses the same machine to alter a document that was used to create the document in the first place, because the typeface and any other individual characteristics would be the same. However, when a page is placed into a typewriter for the second time, often the alignment is slightly off. A document examiner can place a specially made glass plate with an etched grid pattern over the page to check for any imperfections in the alignment, even though they may be only slight.

The typeface of a typewriter

How Forgers Dupe
Document Examiners

Kujau got away with his forgeries by cleverly getting his earliest forged works, his so-called "rare finds," into the collections of the West German Federal Archives, perhaps assuming that any future forgeries would compare his handwriting with those in the archival collections. However, he did not try to disguise his ink or use paper from the past that would have disguised his forgeries even more.

Unfortunately, sometimes criminals can artificially age ink through a process called *oxidation*, using a chemical agent to add oxygen to the ink to change its properties and appearance. If done correctly, even skilled document examiners may not be able to tell if a document has been artificially aged. It takes a very clever and skilled document examiner to uncover the truth of forged "ancient" documents. It took one of the best document examiners to uncover the work of a forger whose skill at aging documents eventually led to murder.

CHAPTER 5

CRIMINAL INVESTIGATIONS: A FORGER DRIVEN TO MURDER

The discovery that the Hitler diaries were fakes happened not through handwriting analysis but in the forensics lab. The diaries contained blankophor, a substance in paper that wasn't manufactured until the 1950s, long after Hitler's death in 1945. Unfortunately for Kujau, although his handwriting forgeries had thus far made him rich, it was the content of the paper that eventually gave him away.

A few years later, however, another famous forger, Mark Hofmann of Holladay, Utah, a suburb of Salt Lake City, managed to fool even the FBI into believing that his religious and literary documents from the past were authentic. Hofmann was a dealer in ancient documents and manuscripts who had sold many famous documents from such noteworthy authors as Emily Dickinson, Mark Twain, and Charles Dickens. He had also "discovered" a religious document that—if authentic—would have exposed some very unpleasant aspects of the history of the Mormon Church. Religious elders in the church had purchased this document, known as the Salamander Letter, in the hopes of keeping this "history" a secret. Later, the church also agreed to purchase a set of documents called the McLellin Collection, which Hofmann was supposed to deliver in October 1985.

Unfortunately, Hofmann's business dealings had started to sour, and he had not been able to either find or forge a copy of the McLellin Collection. In the fear that he would be discovered as a fraud, he resorted to violence and murder.

On the morning that Hofmann was supposed to turn over the McLellin Collection, the police in Salt Lake City were summoned to an office building to check out an explosion that had occurred on the building's sixth floor. A bomb squad entered the building first to secure it and make sure there were no more bombs. After that, the police found a single victim, a man later identified as Steve Christensen, in the hallway where the explosion occurred.

According to Katherine Ramsland in her article "The Mormon Forgery Murders," the sixth-floor hallway looked as though several bombs had gone off: a doorframe was torn apart, the ceiling had crashed down in one area, walls had collapsed, and pieces of plasterboard lay everywhere. Yet after a brief search, the bomb squad realized that only one very powerful bomb had exploded. The victim of the bomb lay face down with debris covering him. His right thigh was torn open through his pants, shrapnel from the bomb had ripped right through his chest cavity, and one of several nails that had been placed with the bomb had flown through his eye and pierced his brain, killing him.

Shortly after the detectives arrived on the crime scene, another bomb exploded, this time in Holladay. The bomb killed Kathy Sheets, a fifty-year-

Bombs may be constructed from everyday parts.

old grandmother. A package addressed to her husband, Gary Sheets, had been left that morning on a wooden walkway near their garage. When Kathy picked it up to move it into the house, it exploded, killing her almost instantly.

Who Sent the Bombs—And Why?

The news of the second bomb mystified investigators, though it didn't take long to discover that the same person had made both bombs. Although

bombs tend to destroy evidence, most pieces of the bomb can be collected from the crime scene and reconstructed. When the investigators did so, they discovered that the bombs had been similarly manufactured, with the main difference being that the first bomb had additional nails placed inside the package and the second bomb had none. However, both bombs were set with a **mercury switch** to activate the explosion, and it looked like both packages had been addressed, one to Steve Christensen and the other to Gary Sheets, in the same felt-tip black marker. The second bomb had obviously not reached its intended victim, killing Sheets' wife instead, but investigators were able to start piecing together clues.

The Mark Hofmann controversy centered around the Mormon Church in Salt Lake City.

One of their first tasks was to find a motive for the bombings. In other words, why were Gary Sheets and Steve Christensen targeted? They soon found out that Christensen was an official in the Church of Jesus Christ of the Latter-Day Saints—the Mormons. That morning he had been scheduled to attend a meeting with church officials over a rare collection of Mormon Church documents.

Many people believed that Christensen could have been targeted over his role in helping the church acquire religious documents. After all, he'd helped the church purchase the Salamander Letter in 1984. Information contained in the Salamander Letter had not been publicly disclosed because it offered an alternate—and not very pleasant—view of the Mormon Church's founder, Joseph Smith. In short, the letter accused Smith of engaging in illegal and immoral activities in order to acquire money. This was certainly information the church wanted to keep quiet. However, news that the letter had been discovered and purchased by the church had somehow leaked to more **radical** and ***fundamentalist splinter groups*** of the Mormon Church, and members of those groups weren't too happy about its existence.

The church assured investigators that Christensen couldn't have been targeted over the Salamander Letter or any other documents he had helped the church acquire. At first glance, Gary Sheets seemed to have no connection to the document deals. The connection seemed to be based on a failed business venture between Gary Sheets and Steve Christensen. In fact, this had been Hofmann's plan from the beginning—to fool investigators into believing that the bombs had something to do with Christensen's business dealings with Sheets. Gary Sheets stood to receive a large insurance settlement after Christensen's death, so this certainly could have been a motive. Investigators therefore entertained the idea that Sheets may have planted

the bomb at his own residence to make it look like he was a target, when in fact he was the culprit. These clues led to Sheets becoming the first suspect.

The next afternoon, as a florist delivered flowers around Salt Lake City, he heard an explosion from a nearby car. Mark Hofmann had been in his car, fiddling with another bomb, when it inadvertently exploded. Luckily for him, he survived with just a few injuries, including a missing finger. At first, he was thought to be the third victim of the bombings, but when he was brought to the hospital, he was unaccountably evasive about what happened and where he'd been that morning. He said he'd seen a package sitting in his car, and when he went to move it, it exploded. Investigators later discovered this wasn't true because of the position of the bomb when

Forensic examiners can extract clues from even burned or charred documents.

Checking Burned or Charred Documents

In the trunk of Hofmann's car was a bunch of documents that had burned in the explosion. The investigators may have been able to still read the documents if they hadn't been subsequently drenched by fire hoses. As it stands, they were unable to use the papers.

Burning documents to conceal a crime is fairly common; most people believe that once evidence of their crimes has turned to ash, they will not be discovered. However, with special equipment, document examiners can often still read what's on a burned or charred document.

In order to do this, the crime-scene investigators need to carefully preserve the burned document either by leaving it in the container in which it was burned or by placing the document between two plates of glass. At the crime lab, document examiners will look at it under infrared light. Burnt ink or pencil marks reflect a wavelength different from that of burnt paper; the examiner can therefore usually read much of the writing.

it exploded. Hofmann said the package was between the front seats, but investigators believed that the package could have only been in the backseat. Also, Hofmann claimed he was in his car with the door closed, but if that had been the case, the roof of the car most certainly would have blown off, and Hofmann would not have survived. Eyewitnesses, such as the florist, said they saw Hofmann in the car with the door open.

Soon after, investigators learned that Hofmann was a rare document dealer and that he had a scheduled meeting with Christensen the day before to turn over a group of documents known as the McLellin Collection. The documents were to have been turned over to the church once Hofmann took possession of them. The meeting had been rescheduled for the next day, the day Hofmann's own bomb exploded in his car. Because of Hofmann's lies regarding the third bomb, he became the prime suspect.

Investigators now knew that the documents were somehow involved in the bombings, but they didn't know to what extent. They soon learned that Hofmann was in serious debt, that the church had loaned him money to acquire the McLellin Collection, that Christensen had vouched for him, and that the loan had expired and both the church and the bank were nervous. Since the church had earlier purchased the controversial Salamander Letter from Hofmann as well as several other documents allegedly written by Joseph Smith, they agreed to hand them over to the FBI for analysis.

Meanwhile, investigators continued to search for a motive for the bombings. They were fairly certain Hofmann was responsible, but they couldn't figure out why he did it or how Gary Sheets was involved. After all, Hofmann was a young, well-respected businessman in Salt Lake City, well known around the country as someone who found rare documents. He had a wife and children, and a nice new home in the suburbs. He didn't seem like a candidate for murderer, yet the evidence was stacking up against him.

Investigators were able to obtain search warrants for Hofmann's residence and car, but the warrants specified they were only allowed to look for bombs or bomb-making materials, as well as a green letter-less "letter" jacket turned inside out that witnesses to the bombings had said they'd seen a man wearing. When the police entered Hofmann's home, they found bomb-making materials, and in the closet, they also found a green letter jacket, turned inside out just as the witnesses had described it.

Investigators next searched Hofmann's van and seized it for possible traces of the bombs. Inside was a receipt for a copy of the *Oath of a Freeman*, another rare document Hofmann had forged, and a grain of smokeless gunpowder like the kind used in bomb-making. They also found a copy of *The Anarchist Cookbook*, which includes information on the construction of pipe bombs.

Investigators still, however, did not have a motive for the bombings. They obtained another search warrant for his home and removed felt-tipped pens like those used to address the bomb packages, as well as wires, drill bits, and other items that can be used in the construction of bombs. Meanwhile, another team of detectives started to piece together Mark Hofmann's complex document dealing.

Two questioned document examiners eventually cracked the case, Special Agent George Throckmorton from the attorney general's office, who first read about the story in the newspapers, and document examiner Bill Flynn from Arizona. After reading about the case, Throckmorton felt certain

Search Warrants

When detectives need to investigate someone they suspect has committed a crime, sometimes they can search the suspect's home, office, or other personal property—but they must first obtain a search warrant. This is a document police acquire from a judge before entering a person's home to search it. Once they have a warrant, they can enter the home using force as necessary.

The Anarchist Cookbook

The Anarchist Cookbook has found its way into the hands of many young people who have tried to make bombs and explosives and ended up losing limbs or even their lives. According to people who know explosives, the book contains many dangerous errors and formulas that are likely to hurt someone following the erroneous directions.

Interestingly, the author, William Powell, has posted information about the book and his views on Amazon.com. He states: "*The Anarchist Cookbook* was written during 1968 and part of 1969 soon after I graduated from high school. At the time, I was 19 years old and the Vietnam War and the so-called 'counter culture movement' were at their height. . . . The book, in many respects, was a misguided product of my adolescent anger at the prospect of being drafted and sent to Vietnam to fight in a war that I did not believe in."

He goes on to explain how after he finally found a publisher for it, the publisher took the copyright away from the author. Powell eventually got married and became a father, and his views on violence changed from his beliefs in the late 1960s. He writes: "The central idea to the book was that violence is an acceptable means to bring about political change. I no longer agree with this." He now would like the book to be taken out of print, but the publisher has refused.

Fast Fact

The Oath of a Freeman is supposedly the first document printed on an American printing press, in Cambridge, Massachusetts, in 1638. There is no known copy of this document. Mark Hofmann forged a copy and offered it to the Library of Congress for 1.5 million dollars.

that something was not quite right in the authentication process for the Salamander Letter. He knew that other document experts sometimes offered inconclusive statements because the ink or paper could be "consistent" with the right type for the age; still, Throckmorton asked a dealer he knew if he could see some of Hofmann's documents to perform his own tests on them.

The first thing Throckmorton examined were three letters allegedly from church founder Joseph Smith, all written from prison on the same day. Throckmorton immediately noted that the letters were different from one another in a number of ways. First, the letters were on different paper, and a different writing instrument and different ink had been used for each one. Furthermore, the handwriting didn't match. Throckmorton knew that a man writing three letters on the same day from a jail in Illinois in 1844 would not have used, let alone had access to, different papers, inks, and writing instruments. Different dealers had probably authenticated each letter individually, without comparisons made, because another expert would have spotted these elementary flaws.

Throckmorton next examined letters and documents purportedly written by three different authors and saw similarities in the handwriting. He felt sure these letters were forgeries, which could mean that many of Hofmann's other sales were forgeries as well. He set out to discover the truth.

At this point in his investigation, Throckmorton enlisted the help of Bill Flynn, and together they set about figuring out Hofmann's handiwork. One thing that helped them along in their examination was a book taken during a search of Hofmann's home, *Great Forgers and Famous Fakes* by Charles Hamilton.

Using the book, Throckmorton and Flynn figured out the recipe and method Hofmann had used for making iron gall ink that had so far defied tests for determining its age. Comparing Hofmann's documents to a control

Because the ink appeared to have run, investigators concluded that Hofmann had forged the Salamander Letter and then hung it to dry.

group of non-Hofmann documents, they also noticed that Hofmann's documents contained two characteristics that showed up under microscopic and ultraviolet examination that did not show up in the other documents: ink that ran in a single direction and cracked like alligator skin. Throckmorton and Flynn surmised that the cracking came from the artificial aging of homemade ink. The downward running of the ink was explained by the fact that the documents were hung to dry. Once they understood this, they could even notice the faint clip marks on the documents where Hofmann had hung them.

Flynn went on to further the evidence against Hofmann by making quill pens from turkey feathers in order to duplicate some of the handwriting on both modern and aged paper. He artificially aged the ink by placing it in an oven, which oxidized it, and he also used a fuming method on the ink in another sample. He found that when iron gallotannate ink was used on old paper and artificially aged, there was no way to determine that it was not as old as might be claimed. A chemical reaction on the ink, if it's on paper of the right time period, shows no difference from ink of that age.

Hofmann had managed to dupe the FBI, many document examiners, and rare document collectors with his clever forgery techniques, but Throckmorton and Flynn finally uncovered the truth. Along with other evidence that piled up against Hofmann, the police charged him with twenty-seven felonies, including two counts of homicide (murder) and multiple counts of fraud and forgery.

Hofmann claimed he was innocent until after his preliminary hearing, in which the evidence against him was just too overwhelming to ignore. Hofmann faced some very serious charges and eventually pleaded guilty to two counts of second-degree murder, second-degree theft by deception in the sale of the Salamander Letter, and second-degree fraud for the McLellin

Bill Flynn, a lead investigator in the Hofmann case, crafted quill pens to study the properties of ink on both modern and aged papers.

Collection. In exchange for his guilty plea, Hofmann was spared the death penalty. However, he had to tell the prosecutors everything and accept a judge's sentence of life in prison.

6

USING DOCUMENTS TO PROFILE A CRIMINAL: HOW THE UNABOMBER WAS CAUGHT

Another man who created bombs and sent them anonymously to people was Ted Kaczynski, best known as the Unabomber. Over the course of seventeen years, from May 1978 to April 1995, he terrorized people, seemingly at random, by sending bombs in the mail, leaving them in innocuous looking packages for people to find, or by hiding them in parking lots, disguised as tire hazards that people would naturally kick out of the way. He even sent a bomb through the mail, knowing it would be placed on an airplane, but at the time he had yet to polish his skills as a bomb manufacturer, and all he succeeded in doing was causing the bomb to smolder and smoke. He certainly terrified the people on the airplane, but he didn't cause any fatalities—that time.

Unlike Hofmann, Kaczynski didn't bomb people to cover up dealings in fraudulent and forged documents. Kaczynski bombed people because he had issues with civilization, namely: science, industry, medicine, and technology. He targeted professors and geneticists, airlines, and even public relations personnel from major corporations because he had strong environmental concerns.

But how did investigators find out who he was? At first, the Unabomber was difficult to profile. In general, "profiling" is the compilation of data about criminal suspects, such as their appearance, traits, and character. This data may lead to clues about their nationality, ethnicity, age, or educational level. Profiling can be based on anything from eyewitness accounts to statistical data, such as the fact that men are more likely to be serial murderers than women. However, in the seventeen-year investigation of the Unabomber, only one eyewitness had provided information for a sketch of the suspect, and, at the time, the Unabomber had been wearing sunglasses and a sweatshirt with the hood pulled up, so he was difficult to identify. Also, his behavior had been erratic; at times, he waited years between bombings. Because his target selections were somewhat inconsistent, investigators had been having a hard time creating his profile. What gave him away was his own writing.

On April 24, 1995, Kaczynski's sixteenth bomb went off, killing Gilbert Murray and making his death the Unabomber's third homicide. On the same day, a *New York Times* editor, Warren Hoge, received a letter from Kaczynski, who claimed he was part of an anarchist group called "FC," which stood for "Freedom Club." In the letter, Kaczynski demanded that the newspaper print his *Unabomber's Manifesto*. He claimed that if

Ted Kaczynski, a.k.a. the Unabomber, sent bombs to his victims through the mail.

the newspaper printed his *Manifesto*, he would stop killing people. In his "deal," however, he reserved the right to "engage in sabotage," meaning he could still ruin property. He warned the newspaper that if it didn't print his writing, he would start construction on the next bomb right away with the intention of killing more people.

After consulting with Attorney General Janet Reno and FBI Director Louis J. Freeh, the *New York Times* and the *Washington Post* agreed to publish the *Manifesto* and split the publishing costs. In the rambling and **pedantic** 35,000-word document, Kaczynski tried to justify his actions by

Using Documents to Profile a Criminal

blaming the victims' own participation in civilized society. The FBI, Janet Reno, and the newspaper editors believed that someone would surely recognize familiarities in the writing and come forward with a lead on who might have written it.

Sure enough, someone did come forward—the Unabomber's brother and sister-in-law, David and Linda Kaczynski. After reading the *Unabomber's Manifesto*, they thought Ted could have written it. The *Manifesto* contained mixed-up phrases like "you can't eat your cake and have it, too," instead of "you can't have your cake and eat it, too"; the more David and Linda read, the more they thought it sounded eerily like something Ted would write.

Investigators seized Kaczynski's cabin in the woods, like this one, to search for evidence linking him to the crimes.

David Kaczynski, although devastated at the thought that his brother might be the Unabomber, enlisted the help of Susan Swanson, a personal friend and private investigator, and asked her to compare some of Ted's writing samples to the *Manifesto*. She agreed that the same person could have written both samples. David and Linda came forward and told the FBI their suspicions.

It wasn't Kaczynski's physical handwriting that initially revealed his identity—although writings found later in his home did match Unabomber handwriting samples. Ultimately, it was his rhetoric and semantics that gave him away. Furthermore, the writing samples given to the FBI by David and Linda helped investigators create the profile they needed to obtain a search warrant for Ted's cabin.

On April 13, 1996, Ted Kaczynski's cabin outside Lincoln, Montana, was searched. Investigators found enough evidence to name him as the Unabomber, including a rough draft of the *Manifesto* and many other documents linking him to the crimes, as well as a completed bomb and one under construction. He was arrested.

After Ted Kaczynski's arrest, his defense lawyers argued that the search warrant was obtained on superficial grounds and should never have been issued. They claimed that anyone with a grudge against modern technol-

Ted Kaczynski's Profile

Linguistic clues in texts such as the *Manifesto* can sometimes help investigators determine the writer's age, gender, ethnicity, level of education, professional training, and ideology. Other clues in the document, like spelling, grammar, syntax, and even punctuation, can also assist in the investigation. These clues are usually taken in consideration with other types of document analysis, such as the type of paper and ink used, and handwriting analysis.

After Foster studied the *Manifesto* along with Kaczynski's other documents, he developed this profile of the Unabomber:

- He was a man much older than the FBI originally thought because he was influenced by New York's Mad Bomber from the 1950s.
- He was highly educated.
- He read texts and novels that were popular in the 1960s.
- He was preoccupied with Eugene O'Neill, a known anarchist.
- He used the sinking of the Titanic as a metaphor for society's blindness and as a way to target his victims and get a message across.
- He tended to take ideas and mimic styles of other writers.
- He searched for victims in specific academic reference works.
- His favorite magazines were *Scientific American* and the *Saturday Review*.
- He was strongly influenced by the writings of Joseph Conrad.

- He identified himself with wood.
- He disliked modern technological progress.
- His favorite research haunts were libraries in northern California.

This profile zeroed in on Kaczynski's reading habits and where he got his information. With this kind of information, investigators can infer other things about a suspect's physical whereabouts.

ogy could have written the *Manifesto*. They asked the judge to throw out all the evidence found in his home on the grounds that the police should never have entered it in the first place.

Linguistics expert Don Foster, who had originally been asked by the defense to argue that there was not enough evidence in the *Manifesto* and Ted's other writings to warrant a search, had refused to do so on the grounds that there was, in fact, enough similarities in the writings to point to Ted as the Unabomber. Foster was then asked by the prosecution to work on their behalf, which he accepted. His report for the courtroom led to the judge's decision to deny the defense motion to have the evidence suppressed.

Foster's goal was to answer the question of whether Kaczynski could have been identified merely from the Manifesto and his other written documents and known behaviors. By studying Kaczynski's linguistic clues such as vocabulary choices, word usage, slang, and professional jargon, Foster came to the conclusion that the FBI could have found Kaczynski without fingerprints, DNA samples, or eyewitness accounts. Foster believed that the

FBI could have found him simply by carefully reading his *Manifesto* and comparing it to the personal document submitted by his brother David— which is, after all, how they *did* find him.

The Unabomber case was not the first one to rely on linguistic analysis in addition to handwriting analysis, but it was the first case, according to Katherine Ramsland in the article "Literary Forensics," that "brought the method most fully into public awareness."

Forensic document examiners are often required to testify in court.

Don Foster helped the case as a linguistics expert rather than as a forensic scientist, but because of his work in the field, he's helped show that contextual analysis of documents can play a large role in forensics. Eventually, a scientific method for linguistic analysis may be developed that meets the Frye or Daubert standards and becomes accepted in all courts.

FORENSIC DOCUMENT EXAMINERS: A CAREER IN THE FIELD

The majority of forensic document examiners don't crack huge cases like the Lindbergh baby kidnapping or the Mormon forgery murders. For the most part, document examiners perform handwriting analysis and forgery detection on a much smaller scale. They work either in private practice or for local, state, or federal police agencies.

Document examiners in private practice mostly examine wills, checks and ledgers, and other personal documents for signs of forgery. They are sometimes called on to assist the local police in other types of criminal investigations, such as handwriting analysis of bank robbery notes or to examine burned or charred documents found at the scene of a crime.

Specialized document laboratories exist mainly in larger cities and throughout the federal government. Several federal agencies maintain such labs, including the FBI; the Central Intelligence Agency; the Bureau of Alcohol, Tobacco, and Firearms; the Internal Revenue Service; the U.S. Postal Service; the U.S. Secret Service; and many branches of the armed forces.

The work of the document examiner is highly specialized, involving great attention to detail. Document examiners must have good eyesight, the ability to work alone for long periods, decent writing skills for writing reports, and extreme patience, as it takes time to follow the scientific method. Document examiners also need skills in photography and laboratory testing procedures.

According to Ngaire E. Genge in *The Forensic Casebook*, the laboratory work of questioned document examiners involves many major and minor tasks. Major tasks, in addition to handwriting analysis and forgery detection, include:

- collecting, preserving, and maintaining evidence integrity in the laboratory setting, ensuring accuracy of incoming reports and information, and accessing evidence
- ensuring the **chain of custody** is maintained
- assessing evidence and determining a proper testing schedule
- performing chemical, comparative, instrumental, and microscopic tests
- examining papers, photocopiers, copier products, typewriters, and computer printers
- using alternative light sources to check inks and toners

A good candidate needs to be:

- someone who is computer literate
- someone who can operate, troubleshoot, and perform minor repairs to laboratory equipment
- someone who can analyze and interpret test results, collect statistical data, and produce scientific reports and **affidavits**
- someone who projects a professional image while testifying in court
- someone who can train law enforcement personnel and provide consultation regarding investigative leads and analytical results

It is important to complete a baccalaureate degree if you wish to pursue a career in the forensic sciences.

Education and Experience Required

While there are no federal guidelines for becoming a document examiner, in order to be certified by the ABFDE, candidates must meet certain criteria, including obtaining a baccalaureate degree and having at least three years of work experience under the supervision of a qualified document examiner. Also, since chemical testing is an integral part of the job, getting a degree with major coursework in criminalistics, forensic science, chemistry, biology, or a related field is recommended.

Ethical Considerations

Document examiners are often called on to testify in court. Their testimony can play an important role in the verdict. Because of this immense responsibility, questioned document examiners must be ethical and use approved scientific methods. They must not allow their biases to influence their findings. Their ultimate objective must be to administer justice. That does not mean that document examiners—or any other forensic scientists—should desire punishments for the guilty. It simply means they should desire, above all, to see that justice is served.

In the article "Ethics and the Expert," Frank Norwitch writes, "the forensic document examiner is expected at all times to be a staunch non-advocate." In other words, his examination should not be biased in favor of who he is working for—whether the prosecution or defense—just because that is who is providing his paycheck. In fact, document examiners should not charge for their services in the courtroom, only their services outside the courtroom. If a jury thinks document examiners are making money just for

showing up in court, jurors may be less likely to trust their judgment. Document examiners' fees should be reasonable and based on overhead costs, their time spent working on the case, and other factors such as transportation needs, laboratory equipment, and other necessary business expenses.

Although document examiners should not merely advocate for the side that is paying them, they should, according to Norwitch, "be an advocate of [their] opinion[s]," and these opinions "should not be taken beyond the scope of [their] limitations." In other words, once the document examiner has formed a professional opinion one way or the other, she can no longer pretend to be completely *impartial*. Her opinion, therefore, should first be formed through following the scientific method, and she should also present her opinion to the court in simple yet scientific terms.

Ordway Hilton, a well-known document examiner, also writes of the need for document examiners to remember that their responsibility as expert witnesses is higher than their responsibility to their clients. According to Hilton, an expert witness "assists the court and jury by explaining and interpreting technical evidence." He goes on to explain that professional document examiners will have examined all of the evidence and taken into consideration any adverse factors that could potentially lead to a different opinion. Hilton believes that if the opinion of the document examiner is correct, and the adverse factors were insufficient enough to lead the examiner to a different opinion, then he should present this in court, openly admitting that there are adverse factors and why he thinks they are insufficient to sway his professional opinion. If he does not scientifically address how he came to his conclusions during first testimony, including the factors that could potentially lead to a different opinion, his findings will most definitely be scrutinized under cross-examination and possibly make him look like he is deliberately trying to hide information.

Code of Ethics and Competency

The American Board of Forensic Document Examiners (ABFDE) has a code of ethics that diplomates must agree to follow in order to become certified. This code seeks to promote the highest quality of professional and personal conduct in its diplomates and candidates:

a. A diplomate or candidate of the ABFDE shall not exercise professional or personal conduct adverse to the best interest and objectives of the ABFDE.

b. A diplomate or candidate of the ABFDE shall not provide any material misrepresentation of education, training, experience or area of expertise.

c. A diplomate or candidate of the ABFDE shall not provide any material misrepresentation, in reports, conversations, or testimony of data upon which an expert opinion or conclusion is based.

d. A diplomate or candidate of the ABFDE shall not issue public statements, which appear to represent the position of the ABFDE without specific authority first obtained from the President.

e. A diplomate or candidate of the ABFDE shall treat all information obtained from a client/agency or through the examination of a document in the strictest confidence.

f. A diplomate or candidate of the ABFDE shall not knowingly perform any service for a person whose interests are opposed to those of his/her client/agency unless directed to do so by the client/agency or by a special order issued by the court.

g. A diplomate or candidate of the ABFDE shall not accept cases where the payment for the services to be rendered is made contingent upon the outcome of either the diplomate's or candidate's examination or the litigation in which the client/agency is or will be involved. Any compensation exacted by a diplomate or candidate shall also be fair and equitable.

h. A diplomate or candidate of the ABFDE will only render opinions which are within his/her area of expertise, and will act, at all times, in a completely impartial manner by employing scientific methodology to reach logical and unbiased conclusions.

Any diplomate or candidate of the American Board of Forensic Document Examiners who has violated any of the provisions of the Code of Ethics and Competency, or portion thereof, may be liable to censure, suspension, or expulsion by action of the Board of Directors.

Norwitch states in his article that if two document examiners have used the same material, they should come fairly close to the same opinion. "When this does not occur," writes Norwitch, "it is safe to assume that only one of two possibilities could have occurred: one of the document examiners either has a serious problem with ethics, or has had insufficient training and is therefore incompetent. There is no third possibility!" In other words, if the document examiners are well trained and professional, if they have followed the scientific method, if they put the ultimate goal of justice above the desires of their clients, and if they have kept their personal biases in check throughout the examination process, they should come fairly close to the same scientific conclusions.

Document examiners play an important, and often crucial, role in the administering of justice. The field has become more and more specialized and technical in recent decades, and it continues to grow and change each year. As a result, document examiners must continually educate themselves about new lab techniques, new papers, inks, and printers that continue to be manufactured, and keep up to date with the laws affecting their careers. For persons who can manage all the technical work involved and have a good sense of ethics, this job can be extremely rewarding.

Glossary

affidavits: Written declarations given under oath.

aliases: False names.

anti-Semitism: Hostility toward or discrimination against Jews as a religious or ethnic group.

apprenticeship: The period of time someone learning a job spends in training.

authenticated: Proved to be genuine or truthful.

authenticity: The genuineness or truth of something.

aviator: The pilot of an airplane.

bane: Something that continually causes problems.

cache: Goods or valuables concealed in a hiding place.

chain of custody: All of the people who handle the evidence from the crime scene to the courtroom.

criminalist: A specialist in the application of scientific techniques in collecting and analyzing physical evidence in criminal cases.

endowment: A grant of money.

ethical: Consistent with agreed upon principles of correct moral or professional conduct.

exonerated: Cleared from accusation or blame.

extortion: The act of obtaining something from a person by force, intimidation, or undue or illegal power.

Federal Bureau of Investigation (FBI): An arm of the U.S. government that oversees criminal investigations on a national level.

forgery: The act of making an illegal copy of something so that it looks genuine, usually for financial gain.

fundamentalist: A person belonging to a movement or possessing an attitude that stresses strict and literal adherence to a set of basic principles.

impartial: Treating or affecting all equally.

inebriation: The state of being intoxicated.

latent fingerprints: Fingerprints that are scarcely visible but that can be developed for study.

legitimacy: The state of being exactly as purposed, neither spurious nor false.

linguistic: Relating to language.

loan shark: Someone who lends money to individuals at unreasonably high rates of interest.

mercury switch: A detonation switch made of a glass bulb containing mercury and with two wire contacts molded in.

obliterations: Erasures or other obscurings.

pedantic: Too concerned with what are thought to be correct rules and details.

penal colony: A place of imprisonment and punishment at a remote location.

probation: The supervision of the behavior of a young or first-time offender by a probation officer.

protocol: The rules of procedure for a particular group in a particular situation.

radical: Marked by considerable departure from the usual or traditional; extreme.

ransom: Payment made in exchange for the release of someone or something from captivity.

rhetoric: A type or mode of language or speech.

semantics: The language used to achieve a desired effect on an audience, especially through the use of words with novel or dual meanings.

special agents: Investigators working for the FBI.

splinter groups: Groups formed by individuals who have broken away from larger organizations.

SS officials: Schutzstaffel, a unit of Nazis created as bodyguards to Adolf Hitler and later expanded to take charge of intelligence, central security, policing, and the mass extermination of those they considered inferior or undesirable.

treason: The betrayal of a trust, especially toward one's country.

U.S. Department of Justice: An agency overseeing many other governmental agencies, including but not limited to the Federal Bureau of Investigation; the Drug Enforcement Administration; the Bureau of Alcohol, Tobacco, Firearms and Explosives; the Bureau of Prisons; and the Offices of U.S. Attorneys and U.S. Marshals.

viscose: A thick, golden-brown solution of cellulose xanthate, used in the manufacture of rayon and cellophane.

watermarks: Markings in paper resulting from differences in thickness, usually produced by pressure of projecting a design in the mold or on a processing roll, and visible when the paper is held to the light.

Further Reading

Saferstein, Richard. *Forensic Science: From the Crime Scene to the Crime Lab.* Upper Saddle River, N.J.: Prentice Hall, 2012.

Camenson, Blythe. *Opportunities in Forensic Science.* New York: McGraw-Hill, 2008.

Campbell, Andrea. *Forensic Science: Evidence, Clues and Investigation.* New York: Chelsea House Publishers, 2000.

Fridell, Ron. *Solving Crimes: Pioneers of Forensic Science.* New York: Franklin Watts, 2000.

Genge, Ngaire E. *The Forensic Casebook: The Science of Crime Scene Investigation.* New York: Ballantine Books, 2002.

Lane, Brian. *Crime and Detection.* New York: Eyewitness Books, 2005.

Lee, Henry C. *Cracking Cases: The Science of Solving Crimes.* Amherst, New York: Prometheus Books, 2002.

Shaler, Robert C. *Crime Scene Forensics: A Scientific Method Approach.* New York: Taylor & Francis, 2011.

Wecht, Cyril H. *Crime Scene Investigation.* Pleasantville, N.Y.: Reader's Digest Books, 2004.

For More Information

The American Board of Forensic Document Examiners
www.abfde.org

The American Society of Questioned Document Examiners
www.asqde.org

The Canadian Society of Forensic Science
www.csfs.ca

The Southwestern Association of Forensic Document Examiners
www.swafde.org

Federal Bureau of Investigation: For the Family
www.fbi.gov/fbikids.htm

Questioned Documents
www.questioneddocuments.com

Reddy's Forensic Science Page
www.forensicpage.com

True Crime Stories
The Hitler Diaries: A Notorious Case of Forgery
www.crimelibrary.com/criminal_mind/scams/hitler_diaries

Ted Kaczynski: The Unabomber
www.crimelibrary.com/terrorists_spies/terrorists/kaczynski/1.html

The Lindbergh Kidnapping: Theft of the Eaglet
www.crimelibrary.com/notorious_murders/famous/lindbergh/index_1.html

The Mormon Forgery Murders
www.crimelibrary.com/criminal_mind/forensics/mormon_forgeries

Publisher's note:
The websites listed on these pages were active at the time of publication. The publisher is not responsible for websites that have changed their addresses or discontinued operation since the date of publication. The publisher will review and update the website list upon each reprint.

Index

Picture Credits

Biographies

AUTHOR

Elizabeth Bauchner lives in Ithaca, New York. A lifelong "health nut," Elizabeth enjoys bicycling, hiking and swimming with her children. She writes about healthy vegetarian food and nutrition for ChefMom.com, as well as the Ithaca Journal. She's also written many articles on women's and children's health issues for consumer and trade publications.

SERIES CONSULTANTS

Carla Miller Noziglia is Senior Forensic Advisor for the U.S. Department of Justice, International Criminal Investigative Training Assistant Program. A Fellow of the American Academy of Forensic Sciences, Ms. Noziglia served as chair of the board of Trustees of the Forensic Science Foundation. Her work has earned her many honors and commendations, including Distinguished Fellow from the American Academy of Forensic Sciences (2003) and the Paul L. Kirk Award from the American Academy of Forensic Sciences Criminalistics Section. Ms. Noziglia's publications include *The Real Crime Lab* (coeditor, 2005), *So You Want to be a Forensic Scientist* (cocditor, 2003), and contributions to *Drug Facilitated Sexual Assault* (2001), *Convicted by Juries, Exonerated by Science: Case Studies in the Use of DNA* (1996), and the *Journal of Police Science* (1989). She is on the editorial board of the *Journal for Forensic Identification*.

Jay Siegel is Director of the Forensic and Investigative Sciences Program at Indiana University-Purdue University, Indianapolis and Chair of the Department of Chemistry and Chemical Biology. He holds a Ph.D. in Analytical Chemistry from George Washington University. He worked for three years at the Virginia Bureau of Forensic Sciences, analyzing drugs, fire residues, and trace evidence. From 1980 to 2004 he was professor of forensic chemistry and director of the forensic science program at Michigan State University in the School of Criminal Justice. Dr. Siegel has testified over 200 times as an expert witness in twelve states, Federal Court and Military Court. He is editor in chief of

the *Encyclopedia of Forensic Sciences*, author of *Forensic Science: A Beginner's Guide and Fundamentals of Forensic Science*, and he has more than thirty publications in forensic science journals. Dr. Siegel was awarded the 2005 Paul Kirk Award for lifetime achievement in forensic science. In February 2009, he was named Distinguished Fellow by the American Academy of Forensic Sciences.